MAGIC ACTS OF KADAMATTATHU KATHANAR

THE SOUTH INDIAN PRIEST WHO WAS BELIEVED TO HAVE MAGICAL POWERS.

JIKKU

Contents

ONE

Ancient Kerala's Some Magic Stories

Stories about the magical works of Kadamattom Kathanar still have a place among Keralites. Perhaps they are all considered exaggerated myths or baseless stories. But in addition to performing many miraculous works of magic through magic tricks and acts, the kathanar has written a book on that art, and one realizes that all those things of the past were not just myths.

It was in this Tamil way that the Kadamattattu Philip Kathanar narrated his magical deeds. Apart from the Kathanar, some of the most prolific "Magicians" are said to have lived in Kerala.All the works of those not so famous magicians were often one step ahead of the Kathanar. But for some reason they did not get enough fame, and except for the rare tricks of all those great magicians, everything else is still unknown. However, below is a list of some of the best known magicians and their hard work.

The crescent-shaped island of Minicoy is probably half an hour long and situated into the Arabian Sea. Also we need to cover210 hours from Kozhikode and 215 hours from Kochi if we travel by sea route.It may not seem strange. Did you know that all the women on this lonely island wear clothes of the same color and shape. The bright red dress worn by all women is worn from the neck to the ankles.It was Ibn Battuta who made a uniform for all the women here according to the rules of Islam. If the fact that the people of the island as a whole are Muslims is a feature, then it is the world traveler who introduces this system to this island , the dress code for muslim women.There, all the men are put kaajal in their eyes. Who taught this routine to them? I don't know .The social life of the people is very different and unique from that of other nations. Similarly, the island, which was formerly part of the Mahal Islands, has a long history of war with the Lakshadweep communities, including the Battle of Sahi.

The story begins when the Lakshadweep is under the Arakkal dynasty of Kannur. At that time Minicoy Island was under the control of the Mahal Sultanate along with the Mahal Islands. The language of the people even today is mahal.

The Sultan of Kannur wanted to subjugate the Maher Islands, they decided to eradicate prosperity and contentment of that island. It only took 14 hours from Kalpeni island of Lakshadweep to Minicoy Island under his rule. It is the island of a few hardworking and wealthy families, whose main occupation is sailing and fishing.Minicoy Island established

Good relations with the western ports. From them Arakkal Sultan learned enough about the Mahal Islands and the Mahal Sultan. Arakkal Sultan realized that the

Mahal island and the Sultan were only within his grasp when the war began. The islands are scattered and they are not very coordinated.

All are small islands, and it is understood that the sultan did not have a good army or other defensive arrangements. The King of Kannur was ready to fulfill his wish.

The Sultan of Kannur arranged nine ships. They are full of fighters. They were commissioned to conquer the Mahal Island community. That small community of cargo ships anchored. They ordered the Mahal Sultan. Must surrender. If not, get ready for war. '

The sultan and the people were astonished, It can be attacked quickly. Some precautions could have been taken if they had known in advance. A few people went and showed their faces in front of the sultan, who was standing in a daze with no way out. They pretended that if we were allowed to do so, we would be able to defeat the enemies of war, and the Sultan gave them permission for the sake of the lives of the people, the good of the country and his salvation.They were a few famous and talented magicians. In Sihar, the magicians were generally known for their magical power. The King would not have been disappointed if the Maldivians had taken on the task of war, which had to be taken over by a willing army or skilled generals.

They started fighting. Eight battalions became omnipotent. Eight Battalions means eight-leaf clover. Good eight-coconut-leaf clover is taken , they prepare it with constant mantra and chants.They also did a lot of writing that would have a definite effect on enemies. Later, as they plunged into the sea, the coconut shell began to sink slowly to the bottom of the abyss. The eight warships of the Sultan of Kannur are passing by as the tidal waves descend.

Thus the eight ships were driven out by magic. But there was still a ship left. The story does not show why it was left behind, or why it was not used for the nine ships for the nine ships. The question is not allowed in the story.The escaped ship immediately returned to Kannur and briefed the Sultan on all the details. In fact he must have been surprised. Where the war will be won if witchcraft itself is used against witchcraft. He asked,where are our witches?

At that time, under the Sultan of Kannur, Lakshadweep, Shakikoya of Kalpeni was the best magician.Sultan was convinced of Shakikoya's ability in the investigation of his soldiers. When they dressed Shakikoya, Shakikoya took the war lead. Sultan sent nine warships to capture Mahalweep soon.

Want to hear about the new ammunition set up by the shakkikoya for the Arakkal troops with eight-pronged coconut shells? Against the sword of the broken coconut shells he used some unbroken coconut. And put some verbs on it.Shakikoya suggested tying this marvelous weapon to a warship and all other ships were annexed to this . Thus an interconnected fleet rejoined the port of Mahal.Mahal demanded surrender to the Sultan and the people.They ordered the mahal sultan to surrender.

But the sorcerers again tried the same defensive measures with coconut shells! This time they must have applied nine scales. After the required work was done, the deadly weapons were thrown into the sea. They naturally began to sink to the bottom of the abyss. But the miracle of the Mahals did not work there.

The courtiers were astonished. In magic, the monopoly monarchy collapsed. They practiced what they learned. But the result was futile. Disappointed by the result , they took up arms and surrendered. The tragic end of the history of deadly magic is the unconditional surrender. But neither side needed a bill, a consultation or a dialogue to curtail war . The total cost of the war between the Kera lands was a maximum of twenty-five coconuts. It is irrelevant here that the Mahal island was under the Kannur dynasty at that time the sultan himself got everything except the minicoy island after many subsequent events.

**Kathanar meaning: priest*

TWO

PAYYANADU KUNJUNNIPANICKER

Payyanadu Kunjunnipanickrr was another great magician who lived in the past .Let's talk about him.

Payyanadu Tharavad belongs to Ernakulam taluk. The family is still relatively high in property and status. That was almost a century ago. It can be inferred from the rumors that Kunjunni Panicker was born in this family more than a hundred years after his death. Nothing is known about the childhood of the panicker. Ordinary people only think that he has seen the depth of magic. Panicker was a terrible alcoholic. People at that time were often convinced that it was enough to please him with alcohol to accomplish anything with him. He used to worship some idol with his magic power as his favorite deity. Panicker performed many miracles effortlessly with this sculptural service, which earned him the immense respect and admiration of the natives. He was revered by all, from Brahmins to Chandalans, even though there was no one at that time who was not unrecognizable about payyanattu panicker. There are some examples of excessive magic of the panicker and non tainted worship of idols.

Karingattu Namboodiripad and Poomully Namboodiripad once had a dispute over a Shiva temple in Ernad taluk. The two argued that the temple was theirs and secured each temporary residence on two sides adjacent to it. The two competed in the annual three-day song festival at the temple. Related fireworks launches can occur on both sides. However, in such cases, it is common for both parties to enlist the help of some magician to prevent the fireworks from burning properly in order to defeat the opponent. At that time, there were some magical Mappilas in that direction. They are often referred to as 'kurus' , a metaphor for making annoying things. If they join on one side, our panicker will save the other. They were convinced that the Mappilas would not have the ability to deal with the panicker. So the two Namboodiris tried to invite him to his side. But Panicker did not have intention to join any particular side.if anyone offer him drink first he surely join that side.Will not be consumed. For a year, both parties started using fireworks while the panickers on the Poomully side and some 'kurus' on the other side joined. The panicker was not involved in any of those attempts, except that he went to the drugstore and calmed down. He had no such habit. In the meanwhile, an ark set on fire by the workers of panicker fell out of a barn made of black straw near the temple and immediately started burning on the roof. When the gardeners were shocked to see this, they said to the panicker and he chants, 'Ha! Went there. Go, go, go, go, go, go, go, go, go, go, go, go, go, go, go! The fire in the barn was miraculously extinguished with the fire, and went back to his side meanwhile fire on the barn miraculously extinguished. Another day, with some application from the people on the other side, the firecrackers and firecrackers belonging to the panickers' party were completely extinguished. When Viva heard that 'Oh it must have touched Mappila. Everything was taken to the pool, washed and cleaned, and then burned.When panicker said, ' Everyone was a little humorous when they heard this, but after taking everything to the pool and dipping it in water When they looked at the fire cracker, it started burning. Look. The great arts of magicians! From then on, the name and fame of the panicker began to spread the country ten times more than in the past. Thus, until his death, this great magician spent his time as a hero in the country.

THREE

ELAMBALASSERY NAIR

Elambalasserry Nair was another magician who lived an altruistic life, gaining extraordinary proficiency in magic, sorcery and poison medicine. His birthplace is about northeast of Pattambi. The history of Nair's youth is not only unknown but can only be understood as small. The name Elambalasserinayar is still revered by many people in North Malabar. With his erudition in various fields, he was able to help many people in various ways, but Nair was not touched by the tendancy to unnecessarily harassed others with magical power. The following incident illustrates how powerful his magic was.

Once upon a time there was a gradual increase in the infestation of rats in a large field near Pattambi.By the time the paddy starts to grow, it can be full of rats everywhere. There was no way to destroy them all without harming the crop. One day when our Nair came that way, the landlord saw him and expressed his grief and asked for help. Nair immediately grabbed a green coconut leaves stick and stood on the edge of the paddy field. After a minute or two, the rats began to appear one by one in front of him and stood at attention. Each of the rats that came near was beaten by Nair. It is said that the rats did not enter the area later. What is the current situation? But one thing is for sure. Paddy is still being cultivated on that land without any problems.

Another contribution made by Nair to the people is even more valuable. The story can be summarized as follows:

At that time there was a lot of harassment of 'Odiyans' in those directions. They was killing people who were hostile to them with the use of some kind of drug.

The name implies that to do some attack on the victim. The assassination was carried out by the Parayars and Pulayars. Some of these (Odiyans) are said to still be living in the wild. Thus, when the persecution of the Odiyans became unbearable, the help of Elambalassery Nair became invaluable to the natives. Nair was not contained then. With a little time, he almost did away with the atrocities of the murderers. With that, it is enough to hear that Elambalassery Nair, all the Odiyans will surely cross the river.

There are many more examples of his magic. We may be amazed to hear that at meal time the tree sprouts in front of the dining leaf and is used to extract the ripe mango from it. But the natives have no doubt in saying this and more about him. They believe that there was no one in Kerala at one time who did not hear the name Elambalassery Nair and it is known that this great magician died more than ninety years ago.

Thus many who at one time astonished and marveled at all the rational thought and outward appearance of the human mind.

Many stories about witchcraft and the many magicians who practiced them have not been published. Is. Assuming that they are scattered all over the place from Kasargod in the north to Kanyakumari in the south and are lying around in every nook and corner, we can go into the story of our storyteller Kadamattam Kathanar's work.

FOUR

A Black magic Application and It's Result

Mar Thoma Nasrani of Enamakkal Church Parish, which once belonged to the Idipranalloor section of Ponnani Taluk, and the Namboothiris of the famous Enamakkal Church had a big dispute over the church. Not only was there no more distance of Half farlong between the Enamakkal house and the church, but the whole place belonged to the house, and the Namboothiri people insisted that the church should be moved from the land of the ellam.

Meanwhile, There was another incident that should be taken as a substitute for this match. News spread that two enamekkals, who were working in the Portuguese fort at Kochi and on their way to Kottapalli, were imitating the parangis and that they were eating beef red and bringing salted beef to their homes, the Namboodiris decided that the church would be demolished from Illam land. The Namboodiris said that they would have to bear a part of the cost of demolishing the church.Nasranis didn't allow this .They were adamant that the church would not be demolished.

The days passed in vain in persistence and and had no decision on either side. When it was finally realized that the Christians were not in the mood to give up, the Namboodiri community began to challenge each other for looking the other way and getting things done. Following that, things turned in another direction.

One day, as the church's chief priest,taking qurbana, was walking west from the altar with the sacred silver vessels containing the deities, he was suddenly struck by a discharge. Then he felt unbearable pain and nausea.Without wasting time he ran towards the bathroom he leftover his divine clothes and sacred vessel.Even when the parishioners thought that the matter was trivial, they felt that the harassment had increased day by day.The incident repeated every time he took qurbana..The Christians believe that Namboothiri's sorcery is behind this.

Namboothiri's sorcery was a reality among people of that time, so what's the solution? They thinking about the solution. They talked about the immediate remedy for this practice of witchcraft . The Eucharist was stopped which was a sad thing for any Christian. It should also be noted here that there was an urgent need that should not be excluded by any Christian. The consultation went smoothly. That's it they searched for a sorcerer.It did not take long for the Christians to find a way. Accordingly, they too decided to seek a cure for the magic of the Namboodiris with a more severe application, for which they immediately send Kanjirathungal Kathanar,towards kadamattathe kathanar . The parishioners did not forget to tell Kanjirathukalachan , the spells of the Namboothiris would continue to recur and that all the necessary mantras had to be practiced properly.

Kanjirathungalachan, who had become a disciple of Kadamattathukathanar, stayed there after learning all the necessary magic tricks within a few days. He soon reached Enamakkal house. Meanwhile the Manakkall Namboothiris had come to know this information.

So, they prepared defensive witch practice. But none of this was understood at all by the Kanjirathungal Kathanar or other parishioners, and as a result the christians generally had the courage not to fear any of this and the feeling that the Namboodirima's witchcraft no longer occurred.Kanjirathungalpur, who has returned as an all-rounder after accepting the discipleship of the famous magician Kadametachan,the main priest decided to perform the Qurbana next Sunday on that courage. But on the appointed day, at the time of the Eucharist, the casa, as usual, would go west, but he would not stop, he urinate profusely inside the robe.He ran towards the side of the bathroom. Seeing and hearing all this made them a dumb witness

he kanjirathungalachan could not do anything. He bowed his head. Achen was relentlessly frustrated and upset that none of his acts had worked. Kanjirathungal Kathanaar stood for a long time in front of all the parishioners like a criminal. He had a great desperation. Other parishioners believed in him and did not have words to say anything .Kanjirathungal Achen's helplessness caused a great deal of confusion among the parishioners. The defeat against Namboodiris was something they could not even think of. So they prepared an alternative plan in their minds. At the same time, they realized that depending on Kanjirathingal was a mistake.

As a result of the thoughts and deliberations of all the parishioners in the aftermath of Kanjirathungal Achen's defeat in magic, they finally came to another unanimous decision. If we need to stop this pragmatism of Manakkale Namboothiri people we need to bring kadamattatachan here.It's only a matter of time. Having reached such a conclusion, they did not hesitate to go to the kadamattam for it.The parishioners who reached Kadamattam with Kanjirathungal Achen inquired about everything that had happened up to that point and understood Achen. Kanjiratungalachen himself had to apologize to Achen's question as to why he did not follow his instructions.

Kanji: Achen - none of my applications work. Namboothiris are great scholars and practitioners. So, it's only a matter of time,achan should definitely come there.

kadamattatachan said, "Nothing works because of your lack of action. I'm guilty of it. It does not my mistake.Is there any women in ellam.

Kanji Achen - Yes. My knowledge is only two. One is the wife of the great Namboodiripad and the other is the married sister .

kad.achen - Well let's do a task

Father ended the conversation by taking a few rocks in the yard, he entered his room and closed the doors.The parishioners and Kanjirathunkal Achen waited outside to find out what he did.It did not take long. Achen immediately came out and handed over the rocks to Kanjirathungal Achen. The parishioners, who expected kadamattathachan to come with them, had some doubts about his work.

parish authorities: It does not seem that Namboothiri will back down from any of this. Heard that they are great magicians. Is it the same in our experience? So things will not end until the father himself comes directly. If Achan herself came directly to our church and did something, they would be saved. If you did not come, we would not be able to live there. The church had to be demolished.

Kad.achan: - "You are not so afraid about that, me the one who chanted this rock, I have used a more powerful defense than namboothiris. It will convince you of the condition. So you must have the courage to carry these rocks and walk. After that all these would be fine.In case of harm, it is enough to take only two of these rocks and throw them towards the bathroom. With that, the whole mass of the Namboodiri dynasty will be over. There will be no need for a third rock. So go with it.

**Namboothiri is a particular hindu caste in south india*

FIVE

THE HISTORY OF INTENSE SORCERY AND IT'S END

Worried by the tragic interruption of the Eucharist, they became desperate more and more.The kanjirathungal achan and his allies described all the matters and also said about the word given by kadamattathachan for helping them. With that, all those faces of despair gradually became miraculously glimmers of hope, and the hope of Aksha's next Mass day returned to their homes.

Now, before we continue the story, let's go back to the historical context of the incident that led to such a fierce rivalry between the Nasrani christians and the Namboodiri.

"It is obvious that all the Syrian Christian churches in ancient Kerala were located within the temple grounds and mostly near the temple walls. Some of the churches were remodeled by the temple itself.Famous kochi ruler shakthan tampuran give his kunnamkulam anthamaal kavu temple given to christians for the church

Adapted from,Chithramezhuthu by K. M. Varghese, Malayala Manorama Annual edition

Palayur Church, Niranathupally, Paravur Churches, Kottappady Church, Kallu Parappally, Purakkattupally, Karthikappally Church, Kayamkulam Church, Chengannur Church, Mavelikkara church , The old church itself bears witness to the fact that it was transformed into a church. The construction of the churches was based on the same evolutionary systems that were later used in Buddhist monasteries and Hindu temples for those whose roots in foreign architecture were seen as medieval in Kerala. Another method was unfamiliar to Kerala sculptors.The Sovereigns of Kerala considered all the ancient Mar Thoma Christians of Kerala as their cousins, believing that the upper caste Hindus here were converts. There are several goals to point out. Along with the upper caste Hindus, the Martho nasranis are also known for their diecrimination against deprived people they considered as untouchable to them.

The rituals of deep bath and punyaham were followed. Despite the hard work of the missionary of Europeans, a small group of Anglicans who remained members of the Anglo-Saxon regime could not remove the immorality of tying knot on wife in the Syrian marriage system, and the upper caste hindus have closeness with nasranis especially the Marthoma Christians, who belonged to the temples of the them were considered as brothers. Similarly, the Mar Thoma Christians had access to Hindu temples at that time . The Nasraniis did not just enter, but also offered sacrifices in temples, sacrificed animals to the temple gods, and attended temple festivals. Similarly, it is seen that the nearest and dearest upper caste Hindus were present at the nasrani ritual Qurbana, which was regularly performed in the church, and Hindu songs such as the Ramayana were sung inside the church to engage in worship with the Christians. The famous Udayamperoor sunnahadose in 1599, the golden ashes of the Sunnahados (Dhatyadi) were kept in their original state. This fact was recorded in the great treatments of Sirmika during the reign of the Englishmen.

Punyaham means splitting water for purification

The Portuguese bishop banned all these rituals of christians, forbidding them from doing so anymore, and thus presupposing most family ties At that time,Nairs it was customary to bury the corpse in large pots called mitavu with christians. May have been obtained in the early days but later may have been not doing this. The cloth and the box were used up in funeral with the arrival of the foreigners. All forms of co-operation and caste are only occasional in the many goals of the Mar Thoma Christians' sovereignty and upper caste hindu brotherhood

No one can deny the fact that this is against the Christian view and contrary to the divine teachings of Jesus Christ. But Mar Thoma Sani was simply innocent in this matter, they follows kings order they follows and it force them to load race, depravity, and caste system.

It does not mean that anyone has the power to violate the law. Violation of customs and caste customs was considered a serious offense punishable. If an upper caste converts to Christianity, it will not be possible to change caste and community customs unless it is psychologically affirmative to the nasrani community. The judgments of the priests, who were obliged to obey even the kings, were also important in this matter. History clearly shows that all the caste transformations that have taken place have taken place only in the wave of political power and in their cold shadow.The ruling of the Synod of Udayamperoor, which took place at the height of the Portuguese rule, and the great defeat of this brotherhood and the irreparable loss of the parishioners with the application of the decrees, are one of the most important events in the national caste history of the Syrian Christians.

That time baptised avarnas faced discrimination.They are not to allowed to marry from upper caste families and did not have right to enter inside the church.The Portuguese army was forced to submit the order towards kings of Kerala against this, and until then the wise Avarnas were allowed to stand in the courtyard outside the Christian churches and watch the Qurbana. The kings of Kerala, who had terrorized by the the Portuguese as a whole, agreed to this reaction. With this, the baptized Christians from Avarna were taken by the Portuguese to the courtyard inside the walls of the Nasrani churches. In some places portuguese cover, mournful chants such as the hero chain, the golden cross, the parangi necklace and the diamond ring are gifted to this newly baptized nasranis.With the help of some influential parishioners, they gradually introduced Christians to some of their parishes. Thus, with the tacit approval of the Kerala Jakans, the Portuguese power erased the Malankara Nazis' aristocracy, aristocracy and arrogance. Whatever their misfortunes may have been, it is commendable that they tried to save the Mar Thoma nuns' cults from non-Christian cults, despite all the other evils about the partners.

There was another mysterious reason that persuaded the Portuguese to undermine the racial pride of the Syrian Christians. In the early days, no women except men came to Kerala from Portugal. In the days before the war, Portuguese soldiers, generals and pantry officers, who were addicted to alcohol, Rebekk and dance, had a desire to marry beautiful Christian women. They tried it in many ways. Through the marriage of the industrialists and merchants of the country to the Nasranis, the second military of them .They fulfilled this.The Parangis had already seen inwardly that Portuguese supremacy could be established in Kerala and that Kerala itself could be transformed into a Portuguese nation. The Portuguese firmly believed that this purpose could be achieved by policy and fear during the period of one hundred and fifty-five years of permanent residence.

But the unilateral decision of the Malankara Christians not to give the girl to the poor who was untouchable to them and eat the beef made the strong Parangis angry. Although the Parangis had forcibly avoid the beef from the diet in the early days due to the compulsive and unethical nature of the beef and also to seek the friendship of christians, they were not able to get married to the Christians. At that time they baptized avarna women and get married or keep them as their sex slave.They gave birth to childrens and portughease style of dress and name were given in abundance from time to time.

After the had plundered the conqueror and inflamed the self-esteem and respect of the Mar Thoma Christians in their own vengeance, they made a grand march into a festive procession to a distant mainland churcn with all the glory of the port power with variety of musical instruments.It has been traditionally said that the Portuguese never carried out such a lavish procession after reaching Kerala. It took about a week for the parangis, who were intoxicated by the victory, to complete her celebrations. In the meantime, the Portuguese heroes received the blessings of missionaries to take dozens of

Syrian Christian women whom they had adopted. Leave out the facts that are irrelevant here as to which section the virgins belonged .

The Malankaranas were forced to make public contact with the Avarna Christians in the market beyond the clashes in remote villages as untouchability was completely lost.

At the same time, they became insignificant in the eyes of the upper caste Hindus. It was a great pain to the Christians that they would allow their own kings and governors, who were so humble, cruel and devout, to allow themselves to be trampled underfoot for the sake of the pleasures and profits of the Parangis. But these close associations with the elite Christians did not leave the Nasranis of that time with the religious consciousness that could bear the immense triumph of Christianity and true humanity. From Manako, they have been willing to live up to the stereotypes of the community, far more than their founder's ultimatum. But they were innocuous. Thus, as the Parangis showed zeal in baptizing the Avarnas and the wise baptized Christians dared to seduce the upper class Hindus in the markets as per the custom, the Portuguese backed them and dared to seduce the Christians and so on.The temple entrance for the nasranis was also denied. As the Avarna Christians imitated the nasranis and entered the temple, they had no other choices without banning both groups. For Marthoma Christians, who were on equal footing with the Kerala class Hindus till the year 774 Gemini 21st of the ninth year, this loss of rights and insanity which took place after a few sunset without committing any crime politically or communally became unnoticed.

marthoma Christians of Enamakkal Parish in Ponnani Taluk, who read in the previous chapter, were the ones who suffered humiliation and persecution from the Sovereign because of the loss of rights of Syrian Christians faced. Enamakkal Church is located in the village of Payyanur, one of the 4 villages of the Namboothiris of Kerala. At the time of this story, there were ten Namboothiri houses in the Enamakkal area called Kanippayyoor, Enamakkal Payyar, Rupayyoor and Vettathupayoor. These are lived in prosperity and coordination.

Of these, except for the present Kanippayyoor Pelakattupayoor Schoor and Vettathupayyoor, the other seven in each period the offspring merged into the adjoining branch of the other three houses. During the preaching of Christianity in Kerala by Marthomashliha, there were a few Namboodiris of the Irimpranallur section and a few Nair families with whom they were acquainted, and some of the Namboodiris, scholars and dignitaries of the Enamakkal house, were among those who converted to Christianity. Illam devi Temple was converted into a church and the cross was worshiped by these Class Christians in the early days. It was barely a short distance between the Enameling House and the Temple of the Goddess on the southwest side of the house. After a long time, the temple fell into disapair . Due to old age, but the people of the parish demolished the Paradevatha goddess temple. The present church on the temple grounds was built about 1200 years ago. It is now a Catholic Syrian Church.Before establishment of the church until Udayamperoor Sunnahadose, the parishioners, Marthoma Christians and the upper caste Hindus of Payyur village, had gathered in a very cordial manner.The news of Enamakkal church courtyard becoming denied to other cast is spread.After that the upper caste Hindus building distance with nasranis .The nasranis are made much closeness with parangis this really shocked hindus they started to fear about their existence this build rivalry between them.

The next day arrived, all Christians eagerly awaited for it. All the Nasranis were present in the church earlier than usual to see the Mass. This time we have to see how the Qurbana will interrupt! It's the only thing that's on everyone's face. This time Kanjirathungal was the priest. This is the first time my father has performed a mass since he learned the magic.Nasranis this time says that Manakkal magic is not possible anymore. But as usual, as soon as his father got up, carrying the sacred casa, he soon felt pain at stomach and and ran to the marappura . The main priest, who was standing nearby, came out of the wall, took the rock from the jars chanted by Kadamattathachan and threw each one to marappura. He and some others looked at it to see what its evolution would be. In a moment of wonder, two very beautiful young women from Enamakkal Payyur Illam, with their colorful jugs and tortoiseshell, come out of their ellam and come to the marappura and wait at the entrance. The people who had gathered at the church were stunned to see this. Some of the women closed their eyes and cried. After a few moments, kanjirathungal stepped out of the bathroom and one woman among them handed Achen a handful of water in a water brass pot and gave cloth. After that, the priest came out and handed them back in the same way.The two women were then dismissed from their caste.

With this, the magic contest between the two ended forever. Manakkal performed the ritual of purification on the same day. Within a few days, the Enamakkal Payyur family moved to another place about twelve miles away with their belongings. Before long, the said house became desolate and all the possessions of Manavaka were transferred to Kanippayyoor Manakkal. The enameling house was left unoccupied for many years and after a few years it was demolished and rebuilt on the north side of the Kariyenthala temple on the east side of the Kanippayur temple, which is located a furlong

*Achan: *Traditional name used by kerala christians to show respect towards priest*

SIX

ELDER PRIEST OF KUNJANMADATHIL V/S KATHANAR

Another contemporary of Kadamattathu Kathanar was the elder priest of Kunjanmadam; he was traditionally a practitioner of magic tricks . In addition to his magic, he was unique and multi-talented even in demonic service. It is said that at that time he even influenced the demons to do his household chores. The elder Priest at Kunjanmadam was a magical king who was so terrifying and practical.The subject of this chapter is a magical competition and its conclusion between the old rival of Kunjanmadam, who was known to be perfect in all aspects of magic, and Kadamattom Kathanar, who had long been famous in Kerala for his magic. This is how the interesting story is told .Although these famous Kerala magicians were acquainted and fell in bond with each other, the innate instinct that naturally arises between two heroes who are equally proficient in the same art was not enough. Although there were regular friendly encounters between father kadamattom philiphose and priest of kunjanmadam, there were no open conversations. It would not be surprising if priest thought that he even does housework with the help of magical powers and how insignificant it was to see Kathanar on the other side of the occult. However, whenever they met, they would invite each other to their homes by pretending to show love without revealing anything like this. But it was customary for no one to accept each other's invitation and hospitality, and to make excuses one by one. But as time went on, Kathanar once thought that he had to gone the way to Kunjanmadam and as a result he was ready for the journey there. But his journey must be a surprise for priest.

If Priest went anywhere, it would be done by invisible ghosts, who would lean on the boat and pull the stern. So father decided that his journey there must have been another work that would have surpassed Priest.When he saw a boat approaching his shore at high speed without the help of any oarsmen or rodman, Priest, who was standing on a wooden porch, was amazed, but when he looked closely, he understood everything. He also guessed that it was the arrival of a strong man who was planning to defeat him, but he acted like I did not know anything.

Aha, is that you kathanar? Glad to see you here , Come with me

I've been thinking of coming here for a while now, but my friend, I just didn't get relief for a while. Today was a day off, so I did not stay. I decided to come out here and father answered his question appropriately.

"Then why did you come out here alone without any companions?" Isn't it difficult to travel without being hurt by thieves and thugs? Potti asked sympathetically.

"Even if it is a little difficult and also if things happen to me in inconvenience, I thought that I should walk forward.It's hard to get a quick punch. But for that reason, it's like not wanting to miss a trip. Achen replied to the elder priest in a trivial manner.

"However, this difficult arrival with the presence of attackers was a bit adventurous. Priest again informed Achen with sympathy.

"Nothing adventure , I did not find the men I was looking for rowing, but I decided to come here. Then what will I do? I got into the boat and fixed my seat. Then the boat, realizing the seriousness of the matter, took me to this place without any hesitation. So I did not have to suffer at all with the wisdom of that boat, His Holiness priest ,Achen replied.

Priest did not fail to realize that Achen's reply was a bit humorous. However, he did not hesitate to entertain Achen.After arranging all the routines and having a hearty meal, they reconvened shortly after. That post-meal conversation went on for a while. I did not know the time had passed. It was about four or five o'clock in the afternoon when my father realized that time was running out. "It's getting late. I'm leaving right away

'Achen said goodbye and hurried to return. "I have invited you so many times, my friend Kathanar, to come here so far. We have the opportunity to meet only a little time each year. So stay here for at least three or four days. Then the return trip was adjusted later.

"Oh, man! Not only that but I have a lot of things to complete, I must go on today. If I failed to reach all are over Achan replied.

Achen told to Priest that he needed to go.

I wanted to ask a lot of questions and understand. It didn't matter because time was running out. So for a couple of days, you must stay here for a while.

"I also want to spend a few days with the Blessed One, but my urgency today does not allow me to do so. I left there,promising to get to Changanassery today . See you. ' After saying this, Kathanar got up from seat.

"What do I do?" Priest said as if realizing Achen's haste.

". I will put forward this if I can avoid it .But this is not the case. I already told them I will arrive today. Father said as he slowly made his way to the boat jetty.

" let it be so," said priest and follows him

Kathanar was suddenly amazed when he reached the boat dock in a hurry following the elder man of Kunjanmadam. boat not seen here, he checked around' But to no avail. His boat is nowhere to be seen. Father kept eye on all four directions for a while. Again the time was wasted and not even the dust of his boat could be seen there. Thought that it was a miracle, Kathanar's eyes went up by chance and he was stunned by the sight of a mango tree standing nearby. Achan realized that his boat was sitting on top of the flour, This is a work done to humiliate him . Thinking that this was the work of this priest that was done with his ghost troops.Achen sent his gaze to the elder priest who was standing nearby, and Priest stared into the distance as if he knew nothing.

A few moments passed. When he realized that Priest was not pretending to say anything, he finally lost his temper and said to Priest: 'hey,Why not move.That's my boat, didn't you see that mango horn sitting here? I used to put the boat on the dock here. It's up to you to decide what to do now.

"I'm not responsible, man! I'm not sure if I'm going to be able to bring this boat down to the river, so you should have to bring it down somehow. I'm just helpless in that regard." Priest looked at her father's face as if he had given up".

Achen was deeply saddened by this empty reply of the elder Priest of Kunjanmadam. Realizing Priest's kind of work,father said to Potti a little seriously and harshly:"Let's have all the work in your hands. I know the thing What should be done.If you did not bring back my boat", I will show you that your ladies will bring down the boat with naked.Mister ,you're dragging me in the wrong direction.

But Priest did not give up,Then let's wait and see

Do not do more to me. Things will get worse, Father warned once again. Priest did not speak at all.

"Isn't it necessary for you to test my ability ?" Father repeated his question.

'Yes'.replied the elder priest firm in Kunjanmadam. "Okay, see, the boat is coming down," Kathanar said, and all the ladies from the monastery began to come one after the other, one after the other, naked, without even wearing a towel. Seeing this, Potti became terrified. Unable to even think of the consequences, he suddenly closed his eyes.

"Enough is enough! Kathanar ,I surrender, I'll give you the boat right now. Do not insult me anymore. Shameless self-promotion of him collapsed and he put a bargain for his self respect.Soon after the boat from the trunk of the tree began to float on air and reached the bank of river.Arrived at the dock and everything was done . At the same time, the ladies who were approaching the boat dock naked were able to run into the monastery.

With this, the long-running rivalry between Priest and Kathanar ended and they became close comrades forever. Achen left Kunjanmadam holding hands and swearing to each other that they would never compete with each other again and that they would be lifelong friends.

SEVEN

THE FAIRY OF PANAYANNARKAVIL

There is notion that ghosts and demons are completely female-dominated. The fairy is said to be the most beautiful devil in that category. But do not think that this is the only complete information about the fairy. What then? She is terrible. Her abode is even on top of sugarcane and milkweed. She's glad when men is dead.Mid night will go to the crematorium and enjoy dancing and laughing. Above all, in the silence of midnight, she appears on the ground with a shapely figure that astonishes the goddess and when she find a men she immeadiatly catch on his neck and suck his blood.After sucking blood she will left hair,nails and bones near to her shelter tree.

Some will believe when they hear this. Others will believe a little. Others will not believe at all. But in the past, on the way to Padmanabhapuram in Thiruvananthapuram, people were attacked and suck their blood like this.Legend has it that the abode of a fairy who lived in there was a reality. Our hero, Kadamattathukathanar, was the one who taught the fairy, now known as Panayanar Kavil Yakshi or

Parumala Yakshi, a good lesson through his sorcery. The legend that is being told about it can be summarized as follows.

In the past, the road from Thiruvananthapuram to Padmanabhapuram was not like today, It was just a one-lane road winding through the bushes, mostly uninhabited. But since there was no other way to get to and from Thiruvananthapuram and East and Padmanabhapuram to the west, the only reliance was on the uninhabited route for people to come and go. That road and its surroundings were enough to scare anyone and there is no need to tell the story of the night.

So, a fairy from somewhere came to here and thought that this place, which was scary with everything, was the perfect place.Would you like to tighten one?" Will be approached with the face of full moon when someone come across the way. Her curly hair, protruding chest, slim waist, and jaggery-like smile and honey-sweet smile are enough to impress anyone, and she invites him to a beautiful mansion. Fascinated by her sexy beauty, he enters the house with her. she appear to be the beautiful young lady who comes in falsely pretending to entertain the guest warmly. Soon she took her nails and sharpened teeth,The man is intrigued by the red-eyed flame flying eyes, the spear-like teeths, and the blood coated tongue ,the hair is stands out thick that stands upright. As soon as her words, which were filled with infactuation, turned to provocation, the poor man frightened and turn into coma.Soon after that fairy eat that man alived.There are so many passengers who lost thier lifes by fell in fairy's attraction.

With the gradual disappearance of many who had traveled that way, some minor doubts began to arise among the people. No human being has ever walked that way after man missing was increases.When the daily prey that was getting from that road was about to be lost, the fairy gradually entered the huts and began to catch and eat the humans. At this point, the people there panicked and began to think about what would happen next. Desiring to drive the fairy out of the area anyway, they brought in a number of magicians and applied all the tricks they had learned. But to no avail. Surplus the annoyance of the fairies increased day by day

The news of this fairy reached kadamattathu priest's ears . Things got to the point where he felt that he should not procrastinate in order to suppress this demon. It was not long before father set out on his journey alone to the place where many of the best magicians had failed to look .

Just before the end of the day, they approached the fairy's mansion on a beautiful evening. As expected,
midnight approached, a glamerous lady appeared in front of Achen, with a shapely robe flowing from the middle of the forest.

"Are there such women on earth?" the priest just said unknowyingly

In the meanwhile, the young lady, who reached near to father, started smiling and saying, "Ah, glad to meet you, father philiphose kadamattom?

Where are you going? she asked ' "I'm going a little east he said. I did not stay anywhere overnight as I had an urgent . I must arrive before dawn.

"There's still plenty of time for dawn. Father will get to the place before then.No need for hurry.Give me a company, did you have lime to tighten with tobacco .Yes I have achan replied,as soon as he said that, father put some lime on an iron rod and stretched it towards her.But as soon as Achen reached out his hand, she started pulling her legs backward and showing fear, he realized that and he moved forward. Finally came to the conclusion that there was no alternative but to buy lime, and she reluctantly bought it,suddenly the beautiful lady became terrifying and achan take her in his custody

Not only did the witch lose all of her demonic power due to her father's cunning, but she also had no control over anything on memory since she bought lime. She may have thought that nail with the lime were given to her. But that was not the case. father chanted the mantra and the iron rod screwed on her head, destroying the power of the fairy and she surrendered to father in the guise of a mohini . So then Achen says obey the way. She has no other options.Achen saw his sorcery win over her and fulfilled his mission. So Achen did not delay his time in returning from the area. On the way back, Mohini was forced to accompany Achen like a maid.

The father walked in front of the girl like a shadow for four or five days in a row. They reached Kayamkulam via Kattanam Pallikkal, resting only in essential places. Kathanar had a relative there. It 's his maternal house . At that time, only his mother's sister lived there,she was an elderly and widowed woman. So Kathanar went home thinking that he could continue his journey after resting there and eating daily routines and food.

The old lady did not feel any familiarity when she saw the young woman who had arrived there following Achen. So when they reached the door, they hurried to find out the details about the young woman with no other personal enquiries about achan.

"Who is this? I do not understand at all?" The old woman asked her doubt.

"Who is this? I do not understand at all?" The old woman asked her doubt.

I got it her on the way towards here.She has no one . She said she is an obedient girl and said that she would do the housework and do it nicely and cleanly. Achen wisely whispered to the old woman, "I did not have the mind to dispose of her.

During this time, the old woman expressed her desire to get her . Is it difficult for my aunt to get a girl for help? But there is no need to worry about it. Achan, realizing the old woman's interest, replied thus. it's great pleasure that I've seen her and remembered that there is no one else here to help me in this old age. The old woman expressed her helplessness.

I know. I can offer her for you.She would be your maid, father opened up.

That's enough. From now on, she too can become a member in my house. Thus, by expressing her eyes

"But let it be so. Stay here with her from today. I'll leave later.

Take a bath in that pool. I will be preparing rice and curry now. ' The joy they felt at having such a girls help in her old age was boundless.

By the time her father came home from the bath, the old and the young woman were already preparing everything for the meal. So Kathanar did not have to stay for lunch anymore. After lunch,father tilted their heads there for a little rest and gradually merged into the comfort zone and fell into a deep sleep.

This our old man and young woman enjoying each and every conversation in another room. After a while, the old woman became very affectionate towards her and desired to tie her hair, so they combed it accordingly. After One or two combing,the old woman felt as if something was blocking her head . Immediately she stopped combing and grabbed her head and slowly pulled her closer to her lap. She kept staring into the abyss to find out what makes the comb blocking and suddenly she find it and wondered 'Aww! Daughter, behold, an iron rod is stuck in your head. How is this happened? Alas! ' Called out loud

When the old woman asked such a panicked question, the young woman answered it like this. My grandmother, I do not know how this happened, it must have been accidentally happened from somewhere. The head is screwed. That's why I'm in pain. What shall I do? '

"Let's see what we can do to pull the nail out," granny said. But I amazed that you didn't feel nail sitting on your head,she pulled the nail away like a spade, the young woman who sitting near to her lap disappeared in an instant.

What! Is what he sees an illusion or a dream? She couldn't believe her own eyes

She was shocked and amazed at what had happened. Where did the woman sitting in front of her go?

The father was shocked to hear the old woman's call and he felt it was a nightmare. Without saying anything, he understood the matter from the old woman's face.Kathanar blamed her for picking the nail on the young lady's head. She passed. Isn't it? ' Hurry up take my cain I will be back.

What can I say? Not even her dust is visible. The old woman replied in amazement.

Anyway it happened. But she cannot escape from me. I will not leave her. Let's see, Aunt.

Seeing and hearing all these scenes, she stared at the road where father had gone,she would not understand anything.

Kathanar quickly realized that the fairy was heading north. When he had gone so far, he could see the fairy speeding away in the distance. She realized that Father was following him, quickly set off on her journey.Fairy is also competing, thinking that he will not be caught her anyway. Soon they came to Mannath. But by the time Kathanar reached the river bank, Fairy had boarded a boat he had seen there and had already disembarked at Panayanar Kavil on the other side of the Panadi. When they reached the shores of Mannathu, there was no boat here to catch the opposite shore. She will cross the river if he is wasting his time searching for a boat and also she will cross the river. He was not a man who did not not give up, suddenly he stand there and think for a moment .A tactic was put in place so that the fairy could not have to cross to other side.Fairy stuck on the middle of the river.

He threw a banana tree leaf on the river and by his magical power sat down on it and rowed it and quickly reached the shore of the panayankavil on the other side. Then the fairy, who was desperately trying to get out of the bow, was frightened and trembled when she saw father coming near.

His father quickly walked over to the fairy and said to her very rudely.

"Where are you going? I will not let you go. If you can sit here without doing any harm, I will allow it. Otherwise I will spoil you. Which one do you agree with?

Convinced that he would not leave her ,the fairy then obeyed him. The terrified lady now realized that things would only get worse if she quarreled with his father. So there is no other way to disagree with it.

I do not want to hurt anyone. So I beg you for my existence so please allow me to sit here

"I swear it is true, I will not hurt anyone anymore and will always be here."

Pardoned and established her on nearby Panayannar Kavil and since then the Panayannar Kavil has been known for this fairy.

In this regard, see the fourth part of the epic of Kottarathil Shankunni

"Although the fairy is said to have lived there, on rare days like blackmoon and Friday, it is said that the fairy is still seen in the form of a beautiful woman and a burning fire in this times.She also known that parumala yakshi.She did not hurt anyone since she got there".

EIGHT

A FAMILY SETTLEMENT SYSTEM

It seems that many people today think that the word 'Kadamattattu' or 'Kathanar' refers to only one person. But that notion is not correct. During the arrival of the Dutch at Kerala,the ruler of Cochin, who had to fight with them continuously, was saddened by his repeated defeats. When the famous magician Kadamattattu kathanar was assembled at the castle, the king sought a solution from kathanar. An arrow was chanted by father, this arrow was used in the Dutch camp by a soldier in Kochi to shoot them down. As he had suggested, they cut each other down and in one night many Dutch soldiers fell. Father was greatly respected by the kochi force. the father appointed by the king as person in charge of the church who was after that no longer the debtor to the kochi. On a palanquin he was moved to church for his grand appointment.The first kathanar was from the famous Attupuram family. The successor are of three generations appointed as priest in their parish church.The pakalomattom thomman kathanar brought his siblings to kadamattom from kuravilangaadu.His brothers iyepe and kuryala settled their and forms kuttapilly family branch.

At that time, everyone was very good at ministerial practices.

* There is a widespread belief that Nasranii priests practiced witchcraft in ancient times. Although there is no evidence today, there is no doubt that witchcraft was known to many of them. That time even after their conversion, the descendants of the Chaldean Syrians, who had converted from hindu became proficient in the sorcery. Philippos Kadamattom was one of the most famous magicians in Kerala who lived in the middle of the 7th century. He not only practices witchcraft but also many innovative mantras have been written and composed. Some of the mantras still used by Hindus today were composed by him.

"Those who have adopted the tactics are still known as the kadamattom follower"

NINE

A JEWISH MAN AND KADAMATTATTU PRIEST

Once a jewish priest came to visit Kerala. On that day, he accidentally went to a church in Kadamattam with the group that traveled all over Kerala. The accidental arrival of a distinguished guest greatly delighted the people there. As a result, The bawa welcomed by church with some rare precious items as a gift for him.Father greeted the audience and started to treat them, there was something special about those presents. It's nothing else. It means that it did not have any of the goods found anywhere in Kerala except in European countries. This feature, which was seen in the visual materials, did not go unnoticed by Bawa at first.

"Father, I needed some more grapes in this bunch. Isn't there one more item that's hard to find easily available in this country? Then the dining table will over," Bawa said with a glance at the material as a whole.

“The fact is that there is nothing on this planet that is hard to find here. If you want green grapes, this invitation will be here too. But one thing is for sure, there must be time to dig up a grape. Just need time to bury it and wait a little bit. Then we can get as many grapes as we want from it.

“Then I want to see. Bawa, who was curious about Father’s reply, expressed his desire.

Okay I will show you,father did not hesitate to take a grape and dig it in the courtyard in the presence of Bawa.

While Bawa was staring at it for the next moment, dugged grapes began to sprout miraculously. Gradually it grew and matured into a large vine within a short time and then had innumerable grapes in it and it all happened in an instant. Seeing this, Bawa, who was shocked to see this, immediately plucked a bunch of green grapes from it and tested it.He himself could not help to notice that there was no difference in appearance and taste as original grapes.

After all this incident, Bawa left the church to say goodbye. Then someone went to Bawa and told him all the details about the priest in detail. The man convinced Bawa that father was a great magician.His house is full of books of Magic ,people saying that eating grapes and cultivating green grapes in a moment was not much in front of his other acts.Bawa also realized that there are witches who practice such techniques. Immediately envious of all this, Bawa went to Kathanar’s house, took all the books that were there and set them on fire. But the result was futile. None of those books had become a fire , as Bawa intended. On the contrary, all the books that fell into the fire flew like birds and just stood in the sky. Even though Bawa looked at all the work he had learned, he could not destroy those books or even a single line in it. Thus, in the end, Bawa himself came to the defeat and had to withdraw from the project unconditionally.

- My dear father, none of these techniques are suitable for Christians. So my father should not do these acts anymore. Convinced that he could not resist, Bawa finally called the kadammattum priest and told him as advice.

'I did not forget God and did nothing to hurt people. I do not intend to do that anymore. It is a mistake to say that learning techniques should not be applied. It is also my duty to fight against whatever harmful things happen to the people. You are trying to dissuade me from it.I considering this as a blessings from my holy father of heaven .He gives a decent reply to bawa's intention

I do not know what to say. If I had known this earlier, none of this would have happened. I'm convinced that what father is doing is very rational and thoughtful. So I'm not saying anything anymore. Do everything as you wish. Let me go.

'But so, thank you for coming so far. I consider this to be one of the greatest blessings of my life. Realizing the meaning of Bawa's haste, Kathanaar concluded his words by giving permission to travel.

"It was an unforgettable experience in my life to be able to meet my father. Bawa also left after anointing father with such polite words in reply.

9 798886 411621

Printed by Libri Plureos GmbH in Hamburg,
Germany